Compiled by
ROSALIE MAGGIO

Quotations
ON *Education*

PRENTICE HALL
Paramus, New Jersey 07652

Library of Congress Cataloging-in-Publication Data

Quotations on education / compiled by Rosalie Maggio
            p.   cm.
      ISBN 0-13-769134-3
      1. Education—Quotations, maxims, etc. I. Maggio, Rosalie.
PN6087.E38Q68 1997
370—dc21   97-35712
                                                  CIP

ISBN 0-13-769134-3

Excerpts from *The New Beacon Book of Quotations by Women* (Boston: Beacon Press, 1996) are reprinted with permission.

PRENTICE HALL
Career & Personal Development
Paramus, NJ 07652
A Simon & Schuster Company

On the World Wide Web at http://www.phdirect.com

Prentice Hall International (UK) Limited, *London*
Prentice Hall of Australia Pty. Limited, *Sydney*
Prentice Hall Canada, Inc., *Toronto*
Prentice Hall Hispanoamericana, S.A., *Mexico*
Prentice Hall of India Private Limited, *New Delhi*
Prentice Hall of Japan, Inc., *Tokyo*
Simon & Schuster Asia Pte. Ltd., *Singapore*
Editora Prentice Hall do Brasil, Ltda., *Rio de Janeiro*

Learning without wisdom is a load of books on a donkey's back.

Zora Neale Hurston

CCD

$\mathscr{C}$ONTENTS

$\mathcal{I}$NTRODUCTION

We can go for days, weeks, and even months without saying or thinking the word "education." And yet, day in and day out, we are educating others and being educated ourselves. In the narrower sense of education—those classrooms and buildings and campuses where teachers and taught are brought together for purposes stated and unstated, for outcomes intended and unintended—we have all been profoundly affected by the pattern of days essentially not of our own making.

At the heart of good education are those gifted, hardworking, and memorable teachers whose inspiration kindles fires that never quite go out, whose remembered encouragement is sometimes the only hard ground we stand upon, and whose very selves are the stuff of the best lessons they ever teach us. Most of us, no matter how long ago it's been, can name our kindergarten teacher. Our first music teacher. Our junior high algebra teacher. Good teachers never die.

A teacher at a large public high school calls his students "scholars" and, over time, watches them grow into the name. An elementary school teacher spends her weekend worrying at the knots of a pupil's difficulties; by Monday morning she has an idea how to unravel them. The enthusiasm of a college professor lights up an unfamiliar corner of the world for students who hadn't known they were born to live there.

The best teachers tend to color outside the lines. They work nights, weekends, and holidays. They buy supplies from their own slim personal resources. Gamblers all, they take chances on students, on material, on themselves. I think they ought to be canonized.

As a bookish child, I wanted to be the sort of person who could bring brilliance to any conversation by quoting well-aimed words from the greats, stunning bystanders with the breadth of my reading and the perspicacity of my second-hand insights. I was sure that all that was necessary was to grow up, that the gift would come with adulthood. It is one of life's little ironies (and not incidentally a blessing to those who know me) that I must still be waiting for adulthood because, like Dorothy Parker, "I can never remember any of the damn things." This is why I collect them.

Some quotations use sexist language (for example, "An educated man is . . ." instead of "An educated person is ..."). What you see in this book is what they wrote. On the other hand, if you use quotations in the classroom, you might want to adapt them to avoid sexist language (as we often adapt quotations for specific uses) or, as journalist and teacher Ann Daly Goodwin used to do, place an X under each sexist word on your chalkboard quotations. The students will eventually realize why some words have been singled out.

This book is dedicated to two young adults who are active players in their own formal educations, creating themselves and their futures as they go. They share the anxiety of many about the overwhelming financial costs. They have forgotten what a good night's sleep is. But they know how to live gracefully in the now; "real life" runs concurrently with education, and vice versa.

DUCATION

If there's a single message passed down from each generation of American parents to their children, it is a two-word line: Better Yourself. And if there's a temple of self-betterment in each town, it is the local school. We have worshiped there for some time.

ELLEN GOODMAN

Our belief in education is unbounded, our reverence for it is unfaltering, our loyalty to it is unshaken by reverses. Our passionate desire, not so much to acquire it as to bestow it, is the most animated of American traits.

AGNES REPPLIER

Education is not a preparation for life; education is life itself.

JOHN DEWEY

Education is not something to prepare you for life; it is a continuous part of life.

HENRY FORD

At its best, schooling can be about how to make a life, which is quite different from how to make a living.

NEIL POSTMAN

There are . . . two educations. One should teach us how to make a living and the other how to live.

JAMES TRUSLOW ADAMS

Every education teaches a philosophy; if not by dogma then by suggestion, by implication, by atmosphere. Every part of that education has a connection with every other part. If it does not all combine to convey some general view of life, it is not an education at all.

G.K. CHESTERTON

Teaching kids to count is fine, but teaching them what counts is best.

BOB TALBERT

Real education consists in drawing the best out of yourself.

MOHANDAS K. GANDHI

Education is not the filling of a pail, but the lighting of a fire.

WILLIAM BUTLER YEATS

Education is what survives when what has been learnt has been forgotten.

B.F. SKINNER

Education, n. That which discloses to the wise and disguises from the foolish their lack of understanding.

AMBROSE BIERCE

Education is learning what you didn't even know you didn't know.

DANIEL J. BOORSTIN

That's what education means—to be able to do what you've never done before.

GEORGE HERBERT PALMER

Sixty years ago I knew everything; now I know nothing; education is a progressive discovery of our own ignorance.

WILL DURANT

Education makes a people easy to lead, but difficult to drive; easy to govern, but impossible to enslave.

HENRY PETER BROUGHAM

Only the educated are free.

EPICTETUS

The classroom—not the trench—is the frontier of freedom now and forevermore.

LYNDON B. JOHNSON

If a man empties his purse into his head, no man can take it away from him. An investment in knowledge always pays the best interest.

BENJAMIN FRANKLIN

Tis education forms the common mind:
Just as the twig is bent, the tree's inclined.

ALEXANDER POPE

Public education does not serve a public. It *creates* a public.

NEIL POSTMAN

At the desk where I sit, I have learned one great truth. The answer for all our national problems— the answer for all the problems of the world—comes down to a single word. That word is "education."

LYNDON B. JOHNSON

A child miseducated is a child lost.

JOHN F. KENNEDY

A life of knowledge is not often a life of injury and crime.

SYDNEY SMITH

Jails and prisons are the complement of schools; so many less as you have of the latter, so many more must you have of the former.

HORACE MANN

In the last analysis civilization itself is measured by the way in which children will live and what chance they will have in the world.

MARY HEATON VORSE

Education is simply the soul of a society as it passes from one generation to another.

G.K. CHESTERTON

Education is all a matter of building bridges.

RALPH ELLISON

It takes a whole village to educate a child.

NIGERIAN PROVERB

True education is to learn *how* to think, not *what* to think.

KRISHNAMURTI

The great end of education is to discipline rather than to furnish the mind; to train it to the use of its own powers, rather than fill it with the accumulation of others.

TRYON EDWARDS

The aim of education should be to teach us rather how to think, than what to think—rather to improve our minds, so as to enable us to think for ourselves, than to load the memory with the thoughts of other men.

JAMES BEATTIE

He is educated who knows how to find out what he doesn't know.

GEORG SIMMEL

Education is to get where you can start to learn.

GEORGE AIKEN

To be able to be caught up into the world of thought—that is to be educated.

EDITH HAMILTON

Being educated means to prefer the best not only to the worst but to the second best.

WILLIAM LYON PHELPS

The most important motive for work in the school and in life is the pleasure in work, pleasure in its result and the knowledge of the value of the result to the community. . . . I have known children who preferred schooltime to vacation.

ALBERT EINSTEIN

A school should be the most beautiful place in every town and village—so beautiful that the punishment for undutiful children should be that they should be debarred from going to school the following day.

OSCAR WILDE

If we succeed in giving the love of learning, the learning itself is sure to follow.

JOHN LUBBOCK

The close observer soon discovers that the teacher's task is not to implant facts but to place the subject to be learned in front of the learner and, through sympathy, emotion, imagination, and patience, to awaken in the learner the restless drive for answers and insights which enlarge the personal life and give it meaning.

NATHAN MARSH PUSEY

Education is the ability to listen to almost anything
without losing your temper or your self-confidence.

ROBERT FROST

An educated man is one who can entertain a new
idea, entertain another person and entertain
himself.

SYDNEY WOOD

Education is the ability to meet life's situations.

JOHN G. HIBBEN

The poorest education that teaches self-control is better than the best that neglects it.

DOROTHY NEVILL

The educational process has no end beyond itself; it is its own end.

JOHN DEWEY

Learning isn't a means to an end; it is an end in itself.

ROBERT A. HEINLEIN

As soon as you start asking what education is *for*, what the use of it is, you're abandoning the basic assumption of any true culture, that education is worthwhile for its own sake.

ANN BRIDGE

Education must have an end in view, for it is not an end in itself.

SYBIL MARSHALL

The function of education is to give the student abundant knowledge in the various fields of human endeavor and at the same time to free his mind from all tradition so that he is able to investigate, to find out, to discover. Otherwise the mind becomes mechanical, burdened with the machinery of knowledge.

KRISHNAMURTI

Education in the formal sense is only a part of the society's larger task of abetting the individual's intellectual, emotional and moral growth. *What we must reach for is a conception of perpetual self-discovery, perpetual reshaping to realize one's best self, to be the person one could be.*

JOHN W. GARDNER

From the very beginning of his education, the child should experience the joy of discovery.

ALFRED NORTH WHITEHEAD

Who learns by finding out, has seven fold the skill of him who learned by being told.

ARTHUR GUTTERMAN

The new education must teach the individual how to classify and reclassify information, how to evaluate its veracity, how to change categories when necessary, how to move from the concrete to the abstract and back, how to look at problems from a new direction—how to teach himself. Tomorrow's illiterate will not be the man who can't read; he will be the man who has not learned how to learn.

HERBERT GERJUOY

The responsibility for producing an educated citizenry is too important to be left entirely to educators. Education is everybody's business.

THOMAS J. BROWN

Education is too important to be left solely to the educators.

FRANCIS KEPPEL

Schools are the workshops of humanity.

John Amos Comenius

The value of an education lies in the struggle to get it. Do too much for people, and they will do nothing for themselves.

Elbert Hubbard

We are not asking our children to do their own best but to be *the* best. Education is in danger of becoming a religion based on fear; its doctrine is to compete. The majority of our children are being led to believe that they are doomed to failure in a world which has room only for those at the top.

Eda J. LeShan

No one can become really educated without having pursued some study in which he took no interest—for it is a part of education to learn to interest ourselves in subjects for which we have no aptitude.

T.S. ELIOT

Education strays from reality when it divides its knowledge into separate compartments without due regard to the connection between them.

FRANCES WOSMEK

Education is a private matter between the person and the world of knowledge and experience and has only a little to do with school or college.

LILLIAN SMITH

School is the marketplace of possibility, not efficiency.

Susan Ohanian

Education has for its object the formation of character.

Herbert Spencer

The chief object of education is not to learn things but to unlearn things.

G.K. Chesterton

Education consists mainly in what we have unlearned.

Mark Twain

Children . . . come to school with their heads crammed with prejudices, and their memories with words, which it should be part of the work of school to reduce to truth and clearness, by substituting principles for the one, and annexing ideas to the other.

HARRIET MARTINEAU

The first problem for all of us, men and woman, is not to learn, but to unlearn.

GLORIA STEINEM

'Tis harder to unlearn than learn.

PROVERB

Real education should educate us out of self into something far finer—into selflessness which links us with all humanity.

NANCY ASTOR

Education, fundamentally, is the increase of the percentage of the conscious in relation to the unconscious.

SYLVIA ASHTON-WARNER

To me education is a leading out of what is already there in the pupil's soul. To Miss Mackay it is a putting in of something that is not there, and that is not what I call education, I call it intrusion.

MURIEL SPARK

The root of the word education is *e-ducere*, literally, to lead forth, or to bring out something which is potentially present.

ERICH FROMM

What is really important in education is not that the child learns this and that, but that the mind is matured, that energy is aroused.

SÖREN KIERKEGAARD

The world of education is like an island where people, cut off from the world, are prepared for life by exclusion from it.

MARIA MONTESSORI

We have set "education" off in a separate category from the main business of life. It is something that happens in schools and colleges. It happens to young people between the ages of six and twenty-one. It is not something—we seem to believe—that need concern the rest of us in our own lives.

JOHN W. GARDNER

So far, we do not seem appalled at the prospect of exactly the same kind of education being applied to all the school children from the Atlantic to the Pacific, but there is an uneasiness in the air, a realization that the individual is growing less easy to find; an idea, perhaps, of what standardization might become when the units are not machines, but human beings.

EDITH HAMILTON

Nowadays it seems that moral education is no longer considered necessary. Attention is wholly centered on intelligence, while the heart life is ignored.

GEORGE SAND

The instruction furnished is not good enough for the youth of such a country. . . . There is not even any systematic instruction given on political morals: an enormous deficiency in a republic.

HARRIET MARTINEAU

I have never let schooling interfere with my education.

MARK TWAIN

If you think education is expensive, try ignorance.

DEREK BOK

Education is a wonderful thing. If you couldn't sign your name you'd have to pay cash.

RITA MAE BROWN

A good education is the next best thing to a pushy mother.

CHARLES SCHULZ

Education is an admirable thing, but it is well to remember from time to time that nothing that is worth knowing can be taught.

OSCAR WILDE

Only people who die very young learn all they really need to know in kindergarten.

WENDY KAMINER

The only thing better than education is more education.

AGNES E. BENEDICT

TEACHING

It is because of our unassailable enthusiasm, our profound reverence for education, that we habitually demand of it the impossible. The teacher is expected to perform a choice and varied series of miracles.

AGNES REPPLIER

Teaching is a rigorous act of faith.

SUSAN OHANIAN

Teaching is the royal road to learning.

JESSAMYN WEST

To teach is to learn twice over.

JOSEPH JOUBERT

Who dares to teach must never cease to learn.

JOHN COTTON DANA

One of the beauties of teaching is that there is no limit to one's growth as a teacher, just as there is no knowing beforehand how much your students can learn.

HERBERT KOHL

The art of teaching is the art of assisting discovery.

MARK VAN DOREN

To know how to suggest is the great art of teaching.

HENRI FRÉDÉRIC AMIEL

The best teacher is the one who suggests rather than dogmatizes, and inspires his listener with the wish to teach himself.

EDWARD G. BULWER-LYTTON

A good teacher feels his way, looking for response.

PAUL GOODMAN

It is the supreme art of the teacher to awaken joy in creative expression and knowledge.

ALBERT EINSTEIN

The whole art of teaching is only the art of awakening the natural curiosity of young minds for the purpose of satisfying it afterwards.

ANATOLE FRANCE

The true aim of everyone who aspires to be a teacher should be, not to impart his own opinions, but to kindle minds.

FREDERICK WILLIAM ROBERTSON

The test of a good teacher is not how many questions he can ask his pupils that they will answer readily, but how many questions he inspires them to ask him which he finds it hard to answer.

ALICE WELLINGTON ROLLINS

What is really important in education is not that the child learns this and that, but that the mind is matured, that energy is aroused.

SÖREN KIERKEGAARD

Other people can't make you see with their eyes. At best they can only encourage you to use your own.

ALDOUS LEONARD HUXLEY

The man who can make hard things easy is the educator.

RALPH WALDO EMERSON

The true teacher defends his pupils against his own personal influence. He inspires self-distrust. He guides their eyes from himself to the spirit that quickens him. He will have no disciple.

AMOS BRONSON ALCOTT

Teaching is an instinctual art, mindful of potential, craving of realizations, a pausing, seamless process.

A. BARTLETT GIAMATTI

Man's most human characteristic is not his ability to learn, which he shares with many other species, but his ability to teach and store what others have developed and taught him.

MARGARET MEAD

Good teaching is an investment in the minds of the young, as obscure in result, as remote from immediate proof as planting a chestnut seedling.

WENDELL BERRY

It is well for young men to remember that no bubble is so iridescent or floats longer than that blown by the successful teacher.

WILLIAM OSLER

You can pay people to teach, but not to care.

MARVA COLLINS

Experience is an expensive teacher. All others are underpaid.

ANONYMOUS

Unless one has taught . . . it is hard to imagine the extent of the demands made on a teacher's attention.

CHARLES E. SILBERMAN

No one should teach who is not in love with teaching.

MARGARET E. SANGSTER

As educators, we live in a fool's paradise, or worse in a knave's, if we are unaware that when we are teaching something to anyone we are also teaching *everything* to that same anyone.

FLORENCE HOWE

Educators should be chosen not merely for their special qualifications, but more for their personality and their character, because we teach more by what we are than by what we teach.

WILL DURANT

I have always felt that the true text book for the pupil is his teacher.

MOHANDAS K. GANDHI

What a teacher thinks she teaches often has little to do with what students learn.

SUSAN OHANIAN

Let me say this about learning experiences: they're weird. Or put it this way: what you learn from a learning experience is generally something else.

PEG BRACKEN

Education is what happens to the other person, not what comes out of the mouth of the educator.

MILES HORTON

Example is always more efficacious than precept.

SAMUEL JOHNSON

Education consists of example and love—nothing else.

HEINRICH PESTALOZZI

Children have more need of models than of critics.

JOSEPH JOUBERT

Children are educated by what the grown-up is and not by his talk.

CARL JUNG

A teacher affects eternity; he can never tell where his influence stops.

HENRY BROOKS ADAMS

I touch the future. I teach.

CHRISTA MCAULIFFE

When I transfer my knowledge, I teach. When I transfer my beliefs, I indoctrinate.

ARTHUR DANTO

Inspired teachers . . . cannot be ordered by the gross from the factory. They must be discovered, one by one, and brought home from the woods and swamps, like orchids. They must be placed in a conservatory, not in a carpenter-shop; and they must be honored and trusted.

JOHN JAY CHAPMAN

The teacher is one who makes two ideas grow where there was only one before.

ELBERT HUBBARD

Everyone who remembers his own educational experience remembers teachers, not methods and techniques. The teacher is the kingpin of the educational situation.

SIDNEY HOOK

Nobody starts out as a completely effective and creative teacher. . . . The desire to teach and the ability to teach well are not the same thing. With the rarest of exceptions, one has to learn how to become a good teacher.

HERBERT KOHL

Teachers should unmask themselves, admit into consciousness the idea that one does not need to know everything there is to know and one does not have to pretend to know everything there is to know.

ESTHER P. ROTHMAN

Superior teachers make the poor students good and the good students superior.

MARVA COLLINS

Good teachers cost a lot, but poor teachers cost a lot more.

ANONYMOUS

The disposition for teaching is two percent inborn and ninety-eight percent reinvented every day of one's career.

SUSAN OHANIAN

Reasoning with a child is fine, if you can reach the child's reason without destroying your own.

JOHN MASON BROWN

Just as eating against one's will is injurious to health, so study without a liking for it spoils the memory, and it retains nothing it takes inn.

LEONARDO DA VINCI

Children always take the line of most persistence.

MARCELENE COX

I am teaching. ... It's kind of like having a love affair with a rhinoceros.

ANNE SEXTON

I do not teach children, I give them joy.

ISADORA DUNCAN

When I teach people I marry them.

SYLVIA ASHTON-WARNER

Not just part of us becomes a teacher. It engages the whole self—the woman or man, wife or husband, mother or father, the lover, scholar or artist in you as well as the teacher earning money.

SYLVIA ASHTON-WARNER

Teaching consists of equal parts perspiration, inspiration, and resignation.

SUSAN OHANIAN

Good teaching is one-fourth preparation and three-fourths theater.

GAIL GODWIN

A teacher's day is half bureaucracy, half crisis, half monotony, and one-eightieth epiphany. Never mind the arithmetic.

SUSAN OHANIAN

Teachers who set and communicate high expectations to all their students obtain greater academic performance from those students than teachers who set low expectations.

RESEARCH FINDING, U.S. DEPARTMENT OF EDUCATION

Children who are treated as if they are uneducable almost invariably become uneducable.

KENNETH B. CLARK

What all good teachers have in common . . . is that they set high standards for their children and do not settle for anything less.

MARVA COLLINS

Limited expectations yield only limited results.

SUSAN LAURSON WILLIG

The only good teachers for you are those friends who love you, who think you are interesting, or very important, or wonderfully funny.

BRENDA UELAND

Everywhere, we learn only from those whom we love.

JOHANN WOLFGANG VON GOETHE

Relationship educates, provided that it is a genuine educational relationship.

MARTIN BUBER

Woe to him who teaches men faster than they can learn.

WILL DURANT

The chief art of learning, as Locke has observed, is to attempt but little at a time. The widest excursions of the mind are made by short flights frequently repeated; the most lofty fabrics of science are formed by the continued accumulation of single propositions.

SAMUEL JOHNSON

Teaching must be determinedly slow in pace.

ALAIN

The training of children is a profession where we must know how to lose time in order to gain it.

JEAN JACQUES ROUSSEAU

Improvement depends far less upon length of tasks and hours of application than is supposed. Children can take in but a little each day; they are like vases with a narrow neck; you may pour little or pour much, but much will not enter at a time.

JULES MICHELET

He who creates a desire to learn in a child, does more than he who forces it to learn much.

ANONYMOUS

Knowledge which is acquired under compulsion obtains no hold on the mind.

PLATO

A willing heart adds feather to the heel.

JOANNA BAILLIE

Everything works when the teacher works. It's as easy as that, and as hard.

MARVA COLLINS

Children are not born knowing the many opportunities that are theirs for the taking. Someone who does know must tell them.

RUTH HILL VIGUERS

All teachers need to have the courage of their contradictions.

SUSAN OHANIAN

Men must be taught as if you taught them not,
And things unknown proposed as things forgot.

ALEXANDER POPE

New things are made familiar, and familiar things are made new.

SAMUEL JOHNSON

Much education today is monumentally ineffective. All too often we are giving young people cut flowers when we should be teaching them to grow their own plants.

JOHN W. GARDNER

Helping children to face up to a certain amount of drudgery, cheerfully and energetically, is one of the biggest problems that teachers, in these days of ubiquitous entertainment, have to face in our schools.

MISS READ

Influencing people . . . is so dangerous. Their acts and thoughts become your illegitimate children. You can't get away from them and Heaven knows what they mayn't grow up into.

ELIZABETH BIBESCO

It is as impossible to withhold education from the receptive mind, as it is impossible to force it upon the unreasoning.

AGNES REPPLIER

One can present people with opportunities. One cannot make them equal to them.

ROSAMOND LEHMANN

You cannot give to people what they are incapable of receiving.

AGATHA CHRISTIE

You take people as far as they will go, not as far as you would like them to go.

JEANNETTE RANKIN

The teacher who . . . is indeed wise does not bid you enter the house of his wisdom, but rather leads you to the threshold of your own mind.

KAHLIL GIBRAN

Teaching is not a lost art, but the regard for it is a lost tradition.

JACQUES BARZUN

Modern cynics and skeptics . . . see no harm in paying those to whom they entrust the minds of their children a smaller wage than is paid to those to whom they entrust the care of their plumbing.

JOHN F. KENNEDY

What was the duty of the teacher if not to inspire?

BHARATI MUKHERJEE

We teachers can only help the work going on, as servants wait upon a master.

MARIA MONTESSORI

The task of a teacher is not to work for the pupil nor to oblige him to work, but to show him how to work.

WANDA LANDOWSKA

The greatest sign of success for a teacher . . is to be able to say, "The children are now working as if I did not exist."

MARIA MONTESSORI

The entire object of teaching is to enable the scholar to do without his teacher. Graduation should take place at the vanishing-point of the teacher.

ELBERT HUBBARD

I suspect you of being a born schoolteacher, something apparently rarer in our day than a fine glass blower, and infinitely more desirable.

AMANDA CROSS

Genuine appreciation of other people's children is one of the rarer virtues.

HARLAN MILLER

For every person wishing to teach there are thirty not wanting to be taught.

W.C. SELLAR AND R.J. YEATMAN

Please remember these two difficult truths of teaching: 1. No matter how much you do, you'll feel it's not enough. 2. Just because you can only do a little is no excuse to do nothing.

SUSAN OHANIAN

Those who cannot remember clearly their own childhood are poor educators.

MARIE VON EBNER-ESCHENBACH

The best teacher of children . . . is one who is essentially childlike.

H.L. MENCKEN

A teacher, like a playwright, has an obligation to be interesting or, at least, brief. A play closes when it ceases to interest audiences.

HAIM G. GINOTT

In teaching, the greatest sin is to be boring.

J.F. HERBART

A dull teacher, with no enthusiasm in his own subject, commits the unpardonable sin.

R.C. WALLACE

Whoever is fundamentally a teacher takes things — including himself — seriously only as they affect his students.

FRIEDRICH NIETZSCHE

Teachers should be held in the highest honor. They are the allies of legislators; they have agency in the prevention of crime; they aid in regulating the atmosphere, whose incessant action and pressure cause the life-blood to circulate, and to return pure and healthful to the heart of the nation.

LYDIA HOWARD SIGOURNEY

Do you know any other business or profession where highly-skilled [sic] specialists are required to tally numbers, alphabetize cards, put notices into mailboxes, and patrol the lunchroom?

BEL KAUFMAN

Teachers have power. We may cripple them by petty economics; by Government regulations, by the foolish criticism of an uninformed press; but their power exists for good or evil.

WINIFRED HOLTBY

America's future will be determined by the home and the school. The child becomes largely what it is taught, hence we must watch what we teach it, how we live before it.

JANE ADDAMS

Many teachers ... would like to tell themselves that education can be nonpolitical and neutral. It is not now. It has not been before. It will not be after we have finished with the struggles of our times.

JONATHAN KOZOL

*L*EARNING

Learning teaches you to learn.

JERRY BROWN

They know enough who know how to learn.

HENRY BROOKS ADAMS

A society in which the individual constantly changes his job, his place of residence, his social ties and so forth, places an enormous premium on learning efficiency. Tomorrow's schools must therefore teach not merely data, but ways to manipulate it. Students must learn how to discard old ideas, how and when to replace them. They must, in short, learn how to learn.

ALVIN TOFFLER

The time for acquiring knowledge is so short . . . that it is folly to expect it should be sufficient to make a child learned. The question ought not to be to teach it the sciences, but to give it a taste for them, and methods to acquire them when the taste shall be better developed.

JEAN JACQUES ROUSSEAU

The important thing is not so much that every child should be taught, as that every child should be given the wish to learn.

JOHN LUBBOCK

Do all your learning while you're young, for when you get older nobody can tell you anything.

ANONYMOUS

The intelligence can only be led by desire. For there to be desire, there must be pleasure and joy in the work. The intelligence only grows and bears fruit in joy.

SIMONE WEIL

The joy of learning is as indispensable in study as breathing is in running. Where it is lacking there are no real students, but only poor caricatures of apprentices who, at the end of their apprenticeship, will not even have a trade.

SIMONE WEIL

We don't get to know anything but what we love.

JOHANN WOLFGANG VON GOETHE

A teacher who is attempting to teach without inspiring the pupil with a desire to learn is hammering on a cold iron.

HORACE MANN

We will be victorious if we have not forgotten how to learn.

ROSA LUXEMBURG

Nothing is known well till long after it is learned.

JOSEPH JOUBERT

I didn't really begin to learn anything until after I had finished my studies.

ANATOLE FRANCE

Your education begins when what is called your education ends.

OLIVER WENDELL HOLMES, JR.

As if we can learn only in school!

NAT HENTOFF

Instruction ends in the school-room, but education ends only with life.

FREDERICK W. ROBERTSON

A child educated only at school is an uneducated child.

GEORGE SANTAYANA

Once children learn how to learn, nothing is going to narrow their mind. The essence of teaching is to make learning contagious, to have one idea spark another.

MARVA COLLINS

The ability to learn is older—as it is also more wide-spread—than is the ability to teach.

MARGARET MEAD

That is what learning is. You suddenly understand something you've understood all your life, but in a new way.

DORIS LESSING

That's the way things come clear. All of a sudden. And then you realize how obvious they've been all along.

MADELEINE L'ENGLE

Some minds learn most when they seem to learn least. A certain placid, unconscious, equable taking-in of knowledge suits them, and alone suits them.

WALTER BAGEHOT

I have come to feel that the only learning which significantly influences behavior is self-discovered, self-appropriated learning.

CARL R. ROGERS

What is learned in high school, or for that matter anywhere at all, depends far less on what is taught than on what one actually experiences in the place.

EDGAR Z. FRIEDENBERG

It is hard to convince a high-school student that he will encounter a lot of problems more difficult than those of algebra and geometry.

EDGAR W. HOWE

How we learn is what we learn.

BONNIE FRIEDMAN

What we have to learn to do, we learn by doing.

ARISTOTLE

Practice even the things which you despair of achieving.

MARCUS AURELIUS

If you can learn from hard knocks, you can also learn from soft touches.

CAROLYN KENMORE

Genuine learning always involves dialogue and encounter.

CLARK E. MOUSTAKAS

All education is a continuous dialogue—questions and answers that pursue every problem to the horizon.

WILLIAM O. DOUGLAS

The world of learning is so broad, and the human soul is so limited in power! We reach forth and strain every nerve, but we seize only a bit of the curtain that hides the infinite from us.

MARIA MITCHELL

I think you should learn, of course, and some days you must learn a great deal. But you should also have days when you allow what is already in you to swell up inside of you until it touches everything. And you can feel it inside you. If you never take time out to let that happen, then you just accumulate facts, and they begin to rattle around inside of you. You can make noise with them, but never really feel anything with them.

E.L. KONIGSBURG

A good deal of education consists in unlearning—the breaking of bad habits as with a tennis serve.

MARY MCCARTHY

The better part of every man's education is that which he gives himself.

JAMES RUSSELL LOWELL

The only really educated men are self-educated.

JESSE LEE BENNETT

A self-taught man usually has a poor teacher and a worse student.

ANONYMOUS

Self-education is fine when the pupil is a born educator.

JOHN A. SHEDD

Change is the end result of all true learning.

LEO BUSCAGLIA

The growth of understanding follows an ascending spiral rather than a straight line.

JOANNA FIELD

When someone is taught the joy of learning, it becomes a life-long process that never stops, a process that creates a logical individual. That is the challenge and joy of teaching.

MARVA COLLINS

The man who is too old to learn was probably always too old to learn.

HENRY S. HASKINS

The one who is too old to learn today was the child who was too young to learn yesterday.

ANONYMOUS

Whoever ceases to be a student has never been a
student.

GEORGE ILES

At a certain age some people's minds close up; they
live on their intellectual fat.

WILLIAM LYON PHELPS

One can go on learning until the day one is cut off.

FAY WELDON

When you're through learning, you're through.

VERNON LAW

*I*N THE CLASSROOM

Every school morning some 42 million American children gulp their breakfast, grab their books, slam the front door and dash off to class. Among them go not one but several future presidents of the United States, a handful of future Supreme Court justices and dozens of future cabinet members.

JOHN W. GARDNER

Students do not need to be labeled or measured any more than they are. They don't need more Federal funds, grants, and gimmicks. What they need from us is common sense, dedication, and bright, energetic teachers who believe that all children are achievers and who take personally the failure of any one child.

MARVA COLLINS

Where the school shows that *it* cares, the students care.

JEROME BRUNER

The secret of Education lies in respecting the pupil. It is not for you to choose what he shall know, what he shall do. It is chosen and foreordained, and he only holds the key to his own secret. By your tampering and thwarting and too much governing he may be hindered from his end and kept out of his own. Respect the child.

RALPH WALDO EMERSON

Feel the dignity of a child. Do not feel superior to him, for you are not.

ROBERT HENRI

If there is anything that we wish to change in the child, we should first examine it and see whether it is not something that could better be changed in ourselves.

CARL JUNG

In the little world in which children have their existence, whosoever brings them up, there is nothing so finely perceived and so finely felt, as injustice.

CHARLES DICKENS

Let early education be a sort of amusement; you will then be better able to find out the natural bent.

PLATO

There is a grave defect in the school where the playground suggests happy, and the classroom disagreeable thoughts.

JOHN LANCASTER SPALDING

In praising or loving a child, we love and praise not that which is, but that which we hope for.

JOHANN WOLFGANG VON GOETHE

The deepest principle in human nature is the craving to be appreciated.

WILLIAM JAMES

Everybody likes a compliment.

ABRAHAM LINCOLN

A torn jacket is soon mended, but hard words bruise the heart of a child.

HENRY WADSWORTH LONGFELLOW

The hearts of small children are delicate organs. A cruel beginning in this world can twist them into curious shapes.

CARSON MCCULLERS

A child with an intense capacity for feeling can suffer to a degree that is beyond any degree of adult suffering, because imagination, ignorance, and the conviction of utter helplessness are untempered either by reason or by experience.

E.M. DELAFIELD

Words are more powerful than perhaps anyone suspects, and once deeply engraved in a child's mind, they are not easily eradicated.

May Sarton

A child develops individuality long before he develops taste.

Erma Bombeck

Nothing fruitful ever comes when plants are forced to flower in the wrong season.

Bette Bao Lord

Little seedlings never flourish in the soil they have been given, be it ever so excellent, if they are continually pulled up to see if the roots are grateful yet.

BERTHA DAMON

The process of education is not generally a process of teaching people to think and ask questions. It . . . is mostly one of teaching the young what *is* and getting them into a mood where they will go on keeping it that way.

ELIZABETH HAWES

In the traditional method the child must say something that he has merely learned. There is all the difference in the world between having something to say, and having to say something.

JOHN DEWEY

A strange thing has occurred in America. I am not sure that it has ever occurred before. The teachers wish to make learning easy. They desire to prepare and peptonize and sweeten the food. Their little books are soft biscuit for weak teeth, easy reading on great subjects; but these books are filled with a pervading error: they contain a subtle perversion of education. Learning is not easy, but hard.

JOHN JAY CHAPMAN

"Predigested food" should be inscribed over every hall of learning as a warning to all who do not wish to lose their own personalities and their original sense of judgment.

EMMA GOLDMAN

Schooling, instead of encouraging the asking of questions, too often discourages it.

MADELEINE L'ENGLE

All children enter school as question marks and leave as periods.

PROVERB

As I inched sluggishly along the treadmill of the Maycomb County school system, I could not help receiving the impression that I was being cheated out of something. Out of what I knew not, yet I did not believe that twelve years of unrelieved boredom was exactly what the state had in mind for me.

HARPER LEE

The first idea that the child must acquire, in order to be actively disciplined, is that of the difference between *good* and *evil*; and the task of the educator lies in seeing that the child does not confound *good* with *immobility*, and *evil* with *activity*.

MARIA MONTESSORI

A child does not thrive on what he is prevented from doing, but on what he actually does.

MARCELENE COX

Teachers and schools tend to mistake good behavior for good character. . . . They value most in children what children least value in themselves.

JOHN HOLT

The attention of children must be lured, caught, and held, like a shy wild animal that must be coaxed with bait to come close. If the situations, the materials, the problems before a child do not interest him, his attention will slip off to what does interest him, and no amount of exhortation or threats will bring it back.

JOHN HOLT

Adults look upon a child as *something empty* that is to be filled through their own efforts, as *something inert and helpless* for which they must do everything, as *something lacking an inner guide* and in constant need of inner direction. . . . An adult who acts in this way, even though he may be convinced that he is filled with zeal, love, and a spirit of sacrifice on behalf of his child, unconsciously suppresses the development of *the child's own personality.*

MARIA MONTESSORI

Too often the adult sees the young child as an unfinished creature, as an object of learning to be molded, shaped, prodded, pushed, rewarded, and reinforced. . . . Significant learning always involves the learner as a person; thus, education itself must be humanized, must include the perceptions and interests of the learner if it is to have genuine meaning.

CLARK E. MOUSTAKAS

Children have to be educated, but they have also to be left to educate themselves.

ERNEST DIMNET

If, in instructing a child, you are vexed with it for want of adroitness, try, if you have never tried before, to write with your left hand [if you are right-handed], and then remember that a child is all left hand.

JOHN FREDERICK BOYES

It is a mystery why adults expect perfection from children. Few grownups can get through a whole day without making a mistake.

MARCELENE COX

Perhaps there is something more than courtesy
behind the dissembling reticence of childhood. . . .
Most artists dislike having their incomplete work considered and discussed and this analogy, I think, is
valid. The child is incomplete, too, and is constantly
experimenting as he seeks his own style of thought
and feeling.

Dervla Murphy

A child's business is an open yard, into which any
passer-by may peer curiously. It is no house, not
even a glass house. A child's reticence is a little
white fence around her business, with a swinging,
helpless gate through which grown-ups come in or
go out, for there are no locks on your privacy.

Margaret Lee Runbeck

A child is a discoverer. He is an amorphous, splendid being in search of his own proper form.

MARIA MONTESSORI

Likely as not, the child you can do the least with will do the most to make you proud.

MIGNON MCLAUGHLIN

How defeated and restless the child that is not doing something in which it sees a purpose, a meaning! It is by its self-directed activity that the child, as years pass, finds its work, the thing it wants to do and for which it finally is willing to deny itself pleasure, ease, even sleep and comfort.

IDA M. TARBELL

Students learn best when they are highly motivated
to do so, and despite a great deal of mythology to
the contrary, this motivation rarely comes from
"inspired teachers" or "well-designed texts" alone.
So long as students are cut off from the productive
work of the surrounding society and kept in an inter-
minably prolonged adolescence, many—if not most,
are de-motivated.

ALVIN TOFFLER

Children do not play ordinary conventional games
unless they are encouraged to do so by the older
boys and girls. Children's "games," strictly speaking,
are not games at all. They are the child's inmost
reality! They are the child's life-illusion. They turn
back to them with a sigh of relief from the imperti-
nent intrusive activities of grown-up people.

JOHN COWPER POWYS

I was a very ancient twelve; my views at that age would have done credit to a Civil War veteran. I am much younger now than I was at twelve or anyway, less burdened. The weight of the centuries lies on children, I'm sure of it.

FLANNERY O'CONNOR

There are children born to be children, and others who must mark time till they can take their natural places as adults.

MIGNON MCLAUGHLIN

Being a child is largely a flux of bold and furtive guesswork, fixed ideas continually dislodged by scrambling and tentative revision. . . . All our energy and cunning go into getting our bearings without letting on that we are ignorant and lost.

FERNANDA EBERSTADT

It was a formidable criticism when a student said, "They do not know I am here." In fact no teacher or official does, in most cases, become aware of the student as a human whole; he is known only by detached and artificial functions.

CHARLES HORTON COOLEY

It is always easier . . . to manipulate the child to fit the theory than to adjust the theory to suit the child—provided, of course, one is very careful not to look at the child.

JUDITH GROCH

I realized with grief that purposeless activities in language arts are probably the burial grounds of language development and that coffins can be found in most classrooms, including mine.

MEM FOX

As every teacher knows, it is easier to move a graveyard than to change a district's existing curriculum.

SUSAN OHANIAN

The content of the curriculum should never exclude the realities of the very students who must intellectually wrestle with it. When students study all worlds except their own, they are miseducated.

JOHNNETTA B. COLE

The first rule of education is that if somebody will fund it, somebody will do it. The second rule of education is that once something is funded, workbooks will follow.

SUSAN OHANIAN

There is a lot of money to be made from miseducation, from the easy to read easy to learn textbooks, work-books, teacher manuals, educational games and visual aids. The textbook business is more than a billion-dollar-a-year industry and some of its biggest profits come from "audio-visual aids"—flash cards, tape cassettes, and filmstrips. No wonder the education industry encourages schools to focus on surface education.

MARVA COLLINS

The trouble with most textbooks is that they take the sport out of learning. Their authors have had all the excitement of the chase.

CONSTANCE WARREN

A workbook should be carefully structured, analyzed for appropriate reading level, matched to every student's individual learning styles, and then thrown out the window.

SUSAN OHANIAN

The Romans would never have had time to conquer the world if they had been obliged to learn Latin first of all.

HEINRICH HEINE

Life is too short to learn German.

THOMAS LOVE PEACOCK

Stand firm in your refusal to remain conscious during algebra. In real life, I assure you, there is no such thing as algebra.

FRAN LEBOWITZ

History did not begin when you became conscious.

LESLIE ALEXANDER LACY

Stop watching the clock; time will pass, will you?

CLASSROOM SIGN

If you promise not to believe everything your child says happens at this school, I'll promise not to believe everything he says happens at home.

ANONYMOUS

HE SYSTEM

While the wheels of all bureaucracies turn slowly, in school bureaucracies many of those wheels have flat tires.

SUSAN OHANIAN

All schoolchildren are hostages to red tape and fiscal insufficiency.

ROSELLEN BROWN

The American school system has, to some extent, simply "happened." . . . It has not been carefully planned. It has not been based on a study, either of children on the one hand, or of society's needs on the other.

AGNES E. BENEDICT

The supply of administrators does seem to exceed the demand. Remember: some administrators are wise. The rest are otherwise. Ninety percent of administrators give the other ten percent a bad name.

SUSAN OHANIAN

She spoke academese, a language that springs like Athene from an intellectual brow, and she spoke it with a nonregional, "good" accent.

MAY SARTON

I'm bilingual. I speak English and I speak educationese.

SHIRLEY M. HUFSTEDLER

If one cannot state a matter clearly enough so that even an intelligent twelve-year-old can understand it, one should remain within the cloistered walls of the university and laboratory until one gets a better grasp of one's subject matter.

MARGARET MEAD

Remember this great teaching axiom: only dull people are at their best during faculty meetings.

SUSAN OHANIAN

There is no sure-cure so idiotic that some superintendent of schools will not swallow it. The aim seems to be to reduce the whole teaching process to a sort of automatic reaction, to discover some master formula that will not only take the place of competence and resourcefulness in the teacher but that will also create an artificial receptivity in the child.

H.L. MENCKEN

Our schools face backward toward a dying system, rather than forward to the emerging new society. Their vast energies are applied to cranking out Industrial Men—people tooled for survival in a system that will be dead before they are.

ALVIN TOFFLER

With large industries throwing out the factory model as counterproductive, it is long past time for schools to do the same. I wonder how many adults would do well at dealing with different job requirements and a different boss every 47 minutes.

SUSAN OHANIAN

Mass education was the ingenious machine con-
structed by industrialism to produce the kind of
adults it needed. The problem was inordinately
complex. How to pre-adapt children for a new
world—a world of repetitive indoor toil, smoke,
noise, machines, crowded living conditions, collec-
tive discipline, a world in which time was to be reg-
ulated not by the cycle of sun and moon, but by the
factory whistle and the clock. The solution was an
education system that, in its very structure, simulat-
ed this new world.

ALVIN TOFFLER

In our mechanized society where thoughts as well as
automobiles may be assembled in an automated factory, it is also, by some narrow logic, expedient to
reduce children to those yes-no codes most easily
processed by such a system. . . . When life becomes
one giant data-processing system, the winners are
those with the greatest aptitude for being data.

JUDITH GROCH

It is our American habit if we find the foundations of our educational structure unsatisfactory to add another story or wing. We find it easier to add a new study or course or kind of school than to reorganize existing conditions so as to meet the need.

JOHN DEWEY

One of the chief hindrances to decent education in America today is the overloading of our schools by placing on their shoulders responsibilities which in other times and other countries have, as a matter of course, been assumed by the home.

BERNARD IDDINGS BELL

A school free to concentrate on those services that only schools can give is in a position to do more effective teaching than one that must be all things to all children and to their parents, too.

JOHN HENRY FISCHER

Most schools have more assistant football coaches than assistant principals.

DAVID BYRNE

Education is the biggest business in America. It has the largest number of owners, the most extensive and costly plant, and utilizes the most valuable raw material. It has the greatest number of operators. It employs our greatest investment in money and time, with the exception of national defense. Its product has the greatest influence on both America and the world.

R.S. SLIGH, JR.

If education is always to be conceived along the same antiquated lines of a mere transmission of knowledge, there is little to be hoped from it in the bettering of man's future.

MARIA MONTESSORI

Men and women must be educated, in a great degree, by the opinions and manners of the society they live in. In every age there has been a stream of popular opinion that has carried all before it, and given a family character, as it were, to the century. It may then fairly be inferred, that, till society be differently constituted, much cannot be expected from education.

MARY WOLLSTONECRAFT

It would be a mistake to assume that the present-day educational system is unchanging. On the contrary, it is undergoing rapid change. But much of this change is no more than an attempt to refine the existent machinery, making it ever more efficient in pursuit of obsolete goals.

ALVIN TOFFLER

The educational system is regarded simultaneously as the nation's scapegoat and savior.

JUDITH GROCH

If there is anything education does not lack today, it is critics.

NATHAN M. PUSEY

COLLEGES AND UNIVERSITIES

It is the function of a liberal university not to give right answers, but to ask right questions.

CYNTHIA OZICK

The things taught in colleges and schools are not an education, but the means of education.

RALPH WALDO EMERSON

The primary purpose of a liberal education is to make one's mind a pleasant place in which to spend one's leisure.

SIDNEY J. HARRIS

No man should escape our universities without knowing how little he knows.

J. ROBERT OPPENHEIMER

The university is simply the canary in the coalmine. It is the most sensitive barometer of social change.

JAMES PERKINS

A liberal-arts education is supposed to provide you with a value system, a standard, a set of ideas, not a job.

CAROLINE BIRD

Enthusiasm comes out of the world and goes into the university. Toward this point flow the currents of new talent that bubble up in society: here is the meeting-place of mind. All that a university does is to give the poppy-seed to the soil, the oil to the lamp, the gold to the rod of glass before it cools. A university brings the spirit in touch with its own language, that language through which it has spoken in former days and through which alone it shall speak again.

JOHN JAY CHAPMAN

Academic education is the act of memorizing things read in books, and things told by college professors who got their education mostly by memorizing things read in books and told by college professors.

ELBERT HUBBARD

Universities are full of knowledge; the freshmen bring a little in and the seniors take away none at all, and the knowledge accumulates.

LAWRENCE LOWELL

I find that the three major administrative problems on a campus are sex for the students, athletics for the alumni, and parking for the faculty.

CLARK KERR

I learned three important things in college—to use a library, to memorize quickly and visually, to drop asleep at any time given a horizontal surface and fifteen minutes. What I could not learn was to think creatively on schedule.

AGNES DE MILLE

It is one of the great pleasures of a student's life to buy a heap of books at the beginning of the autumn. Here, he fancies, are all the secrets.

ROBERT LYND

Everywhere I go I'm asked if I think the university stifles writers. My opinion is that they don't stifle enough of them. There's many a best-seller that could have been prevented by a good teacher.

FLANNERY O'CONNOR

Ignorance, arrogance, and racism have bloomed as Superior Knowledge in all too many universities.

ALICE WALKER

Most higher education is devoted to affirming the traditions and origins of an existing elite and transmitting them to new members.

MARY CATHERINE BATESON

We have this mistaken notion that everybody in the world has to go to college.

KATHERINE ANNE PORTER

You are not necessarily educated because you have been to college. Each soul needs a different education. Many a man has been educated by his folly.

ALICE WELLINGTON ROLLINS

Equalizing opportunity through universal higher education subjects the whole population to the intellectual mode natural only to a few. It violates the fundamental egalitarian principle of respect for the differences between people.

CAROLINE BIRD

The quality of a university is measured more by the kind of student it turns out than the kind it takes in.

ROBERT J. KIBBER

If you feel that you have both feet planted on level ground, then the university has failed you.

ROBERT GOHEEN

THINKING

What is the hardest task in the world? To think.

RALPH WALDO EMERSON

Thinking is the hardest work in the world; and most of us will go to great lengths to avoid it.

LOUISE DUDLEY

To most people nothing is more troublesome than the effort of thinking.

JAMES BRYCE

If you make people think that they think they will love you; but if you make them really think they will hate you.

ROSCOE B. ELLARD

There are no dangerous thoughts; thinking itself is dangerous.

HANNAH ARENDT

Never be afraid to sit awhile and think.

LORRAINE HANSBERRY

To have ideas is to gather flowers. To think is to weave them into garlands.

ANNE-SOPHIE SWETCHINE

To think and to be fully alive are the same.

HANNAH ARENDT

Nothing cheers me up like having understood
something difficult to understand.

G.C. LICHTENBERG

Making mental connections is our most crucial
learning tool, the essence of human intelligence: to
forge links; to go beyond the given; to see patterns,
relationship, context.

MARILYN FERGUSON

All men see the same objects, but do not equally
understand them. Intelligence is the tongue that dis-
cerns and tastes them.

THOMAS TRAHERNE

The highest, most varied and lasting pleasures are
those of the mind.

ARTHUR SCHOPENHAUER

It interrupts any doing, any ordinary activities, no matter what they happen to be. All thinking demands a *stop*-and-think.

HANNAH ARENDT

A problem adequately stated is a problem well on its way to being solved.

R. BUCKMINSTER FULLER

If we can really understand the problem, the answer will come out of it, because the answer is not separate from the problem.

KRISHNAMURTI

The frightening thing is their unquestioning acceptance of whatever is taught to them by anyone in front of the room. This has nothing to do with rebellion against authority; they rebel, all right, and loudly. But it doesn't occur to them to think.

BEL KAUFMAN

The best way to get a good idea is to get a lot of ideas.

LINUS PAULING

To repeat what others have said, requires education; to challenge it, requires brains.

MARY PETTIBONE POOLE

People get wisdom from thinking, not from learning.

LAURA RIDING JACKSON

Reading furnishes the mind only with materials of knowledge; it is thinking makes what we read ours.

JOHN LOCKE

Learning without thought is useless; thought without learning is dangerous.

CONFUCIUS

The mind is an enchanting thing.

MARIANNE MOORE

Our progress as a nation can be no swifter than our progress in education . . . . The human mind is our fundamental resource.

JOHN F. KENNEDY

The mind is like the stomach. It is not how much you put into it that counts, but how much it digests.

ALBERT JAY NOCK

Our minds are like our stomachs; they are whetted by the change of their food, and variety supplies both with fresh appetite.

QUINTILIAN

The mind is more vulnerable than the stomach, because it can be poisoned without feeling immediate pain.

HELEN MACINNES

That most sensitive, most delicate of instruments— the mind of a little child!

HENRY HANDEL RICHARDSON

The purpose of education is to replace an empty mind with an open one.

MALCOLM S. FORBES

It's a pity that things weren't arranged so that an empty head, like an empty stomach, would not let us rest until we put something in it.

RED GRAY

The whole object of education is, or should be, to develop the mind. The mind should be a thing that works.

SHERWOOD ANDERSON

Minds are like oysters. They spoil if you pry them open.

WILLA GIBBS

His mind had been receptive up to a certain age,
and then had snapped shut on what it possessed,
like a replete crustacean never reached by another
high tide.

EDITH WHARTON

Minds are like parachutes. They only function
when they are open.

JAMES DEWAR

The human mind is like an umbrella—it functions
best when open.

WALTER ADOLF GROPIUS

Some minds remain open long enough for the truth
not only to enter but to pass on through by way of a
ready exit without pausing anywhere along the route.

ELIZABETH KENNY

A closed mind is a dying mind.

EDNA FERBER

This alone is to be feared—the closed mind, the sleeping imagination, the death of the spirit. The death of the body is to that, I think, a little thing.

WINIFRED HOLTBY

Mind unemployed is mind unenjoyed.

CHRISTIAN NESTELL BOVEE

It's good to let your mind go blank occasionally, but only if you turn the sound off too.

ANONYMOUS

Where all think alike, no one thinks very much.

WALTER LIPPMAN

As towards most other things of which we have but little personal experience (foreigners, or socialists, or aristocrats, as the case may be), there is a degree of vague ill-will towards what is called *Thinking*.

VERNON LEE

Learning can be a bridge between doing and thinking. But then there is a danger that the person who uses learning as a bridge between doing and thinking may get stuck in learning and never get on to thinking.

LAURA RIDING JACKSON

Freedom to think requires not only freedom of expression but also freedom from the threat of orthodoxy and being outcast and ostracized.

HELEN FOSTER SNOW

My thoughts are like waffles—the first few don't look too good.

MARILYN VOS SAVANT

Once you wake up thought in a man, you can never put it to sleep again.

ZORA NEALE HURSTON

A mind once cultivated will not lie fallow for half an hour.

EDWARD G. BULWER-LYTTON

Few minds wear out; more rust out.

CHRISTIAN NESTELL BOVEE

Thinking . . . is a soundless dialogue, it is the weaving of patterns, it is a search for meaning. The activity of thought contributes to and shapes all that is specifically human.

VERA JOHN-STEINER

Many highly successful individuals have above-average but not extraordinary intelligence. Accomplishment in a particular activity is often more dependent upon hard work and self-discipline than on innate ability.

RESEARCH FINDING,
U.S. DEPARTMENT OF EDUCATION

Genius . . . means little more than the faculty of perceiving in an unhabitual way.

WILLIAM JAMES

A man who is a genius and doesn't know it, probably isn't.

STANISLAW J. LEC

The true test of intelligence is not how much we know how to do, but how we behave when we don't know what to do.

JOHN HOLT

Of all forms of wealth, intelligence at least seems fairly distributed; for no man complains of a lack of it.

SAMUEL JOHNSON

What is reason? Knowledge informed by sympathy, intelligence in the arms of love.

EDWARD ABBEY

He did not arrive at this conclusion by the decent process of quiet, logical deduction, nor yet by the blinding flash of glorious intuition, but by the shoddy, untidy process halfway between the two by which one usually gets to know things.

MARGERY ALLINGHAM

The more you use your brain, the more brain you will have to use.

G.A. DORSEY

I not only use all the brains I have, but all I can borrow.

WOODROW WILSON

The softest, freest, most pliable and changeful living substance is the brain—the hardest and most iron-bound as well.

CHARLOTTE PERKINS GILMAN

The mind, of course, is just what the brain does for a living.

SHARON BEGLEY

If a mind is just a few pounds of blood, dream, and electric, how does it manage to contemplate itself, worry about its soul, do time-and-motion studies, admire the shy hooves of a goat, know that it will die, enjoy all the grand and lesser mayhems of the heart?

DIANE ACKERMAN

The mind is an astonishing, long-living, erotic thing.

GRACE PALEY

It is in our minds that we live much of our life.

IVY COMPTON-BURNETT

The mind I love must still have wild places, a tangled orchard where dark damsons drop in the heavy grass, an overgrown little wood, the chance of a snake or two (real snakes), a pool that nobody's fathomed the depth of—and paths threaded with those little flowers planted by the mind.

KATHERINE MANSFIELD

The different faculties [of the mind] divide themselves in the main into two classifications, which I
call *hot* (the creative) and *cold* (the critical).

MARY O'HARA

When the mind is most empty
It is most full.

SUSAN FROMBERG SCHAEFFER

The mind has no sex.

GEORGE SAND

The mind's cross-indexing puts the best librarian to
shame.

SHARON BEGLEY

When different talents and ideas rub up against each other, there is friction, yes. But also sparks, fire, light and—eventually—brilliance!

NANCIE O'NEILL

IGNORANCE

Everybody is ignorant, only on different subjects.

WILL ROGERS

The world is full of ignorant people who don't know what you have just found out.

ANONYMOUS

The more we study the more we discover our ignorance.

PERCY BYSSHE SHELLEY

The more we learn the more we realize how little we know.

R. Buckminster Fuller

In order to have wisdom we must have ignorance.

Theodore Dreiser

Doubt grows with knowledge.

Johann Wolfgang von Goethe

Doubt is the necessary tool of knowledge.

Paul Tillich

The greater our knowledge increases, the greater our ignorance unfolds.

JOHN F. KENNEDY

Ignorance lies at the bottom of all human knowledge, and the deeper we penetrate the nearer we arrive unto it.

CHARLES CALEB COLTON

The farther one pursues knowledge, the less one knows.

LAO-TSE

Ignorance is the beginning of knowledge; knowledge is the beginning of wisdom; wisdom is the awareness of ignorance.

WILLIAM ROTSLER

They say that what you don't know won't hurt you—
and some of us haven't felt a twinge of pain in years.

FLETCHER KNEBEL

Our knowledge can only be finite, while our ignorance must necessarily be infinite.

KARL POPPER

Stupidity is sufficient unto itself. Wisdom can never
learn enough.

MECHTHILD OF MAGDEBURG

Have the courage to be ignorant of a great number
of things, in order to avoid the calamity of being
ignorant of everything.

SYDNEY SMITH

It is the province of knowledge to speak and it is the privilege of wisdom to listen.

OLIVER WENDELL HOLMES, SR.

One of the frightening things about our time is the number of people who think it is a form of intellectual audacity to be stupid. A whole generation seems to be taking on an easy distrust of thought.

RENATA ADLER

Too many of our countrymen rejoice in stupidity, look upon ignorance as a badge of honor. They condemn everything they don't understand.

TALLULAH BANKHEAD

Ignorance, far more than idleness, is the mother of all the vices.

L.E. LANDON

The most violent element in society is ignorance.

EMMA GOLDMAN

Only ignorance! only *ignorance*! how can you talk about *only* ignorance? Don't you know that it is the worst thing in the world, next to wickedness? And which does the most mischief Heaven only knows. If people can say, "Oh! I did not know, I did not mean any harm," they think it is all right.

ANNA SEWELL

There is nothing more powerful than ignorance, not even intelligence.

LILLIAN SMITH

Nothing is more terrible than ignorance in action.

JOHANN WOLFGANG VON GOETHE

Ignorance is not bliss. Ignorance is impotence; it is fear; it is cruelty; it is all the things that make for unhappiness.

WINIFRED HOLTBY

The bliss that comes from ignorance should seldom be encouraged for it is likely to do one out of a more satisfying bliss.

RUTH STOUT

Most people did not care to be taught what they did not already know; it made them feel ignorant.

MARY MCCARTHY

Those who know nothing must believe everything.

MARIE VON EBNER-ESCHENBACH

Ignorance gives one a large range of probabilities.

GEORGE ELIOT

To be conscious that you are ignorant is a great step to knowledge.

BENJAMIN DISRAELI

The first step to knowledge is to know that we are ignorant.

DAVID CECIL

NOWLEDGE

Knowledge is power.

FRANCIS BACON

To know you know is power.

ELBERT HUBBARD

Knowledge is a process, not a product.

RUTH NANDA ANSHEN

Feeding and knowing are both ways of growing.

IRVING H. BUCHEN

All men by nature desire to know.

ARISTOTLE

A desire of knowledge is the natural feeling of mankind; and every human being whose mind is not debauched, will be willing to give all that he has to get knowledge.

SAMUEL JOHNSON

Desire of knowledge, like the thirst of riches, increases ever with the acquisition of it.

LAURENCE STERNE

We have a hunger of the mind which asks for knowledge of all around us, and the more we gain, the more is our desire; the more we see, the more are we capable of seeing.

MARIA MITCHELL

What we want is to see the child in pursuit of knowledge, and not knowledge in pursuit of the child.

GEORGE BERNARD SHAW

As knowledge increases, wonder deepens.

CHARLES MORGAN

Knowledge is of two kinds. We know a subject ourselves, or we know where we can find information upon it.

SAMUEL JOHNSON

Our biggest problem as human beings is not knowing that we don't know.

VIRGINIA SATIR

Shall I tell you what knowledge is? It is to know
both what one knows and what one does not know.

CONFUCIUS

He that knew all that ever learning writ,
Knew only this—that he knew nothing yet.

APHRA BEHN

I am not wise. Not knowing, and learning to be
comfortable with not knowing, is a great discovery.

SUE BENDER

We don't know one millionth of one percent about anything.

THOMAS A. EDISON

The mind can store an estimated 100 trillion bits of information—compared with which a computer's mere billions are virtually amnesiac.

SHARON BEGLEY

Fifty per cent of what I know today will be obsolete in five years, but I don't know which half.

JAMES R. HICKMAN

The foolish and the dead alone never change their opinions.

JAMES RUSSELL LOWELL

Some people know a lot more when you try to tell them something than when you ask them something.

ANONYMOUS

Nobody knows enough, but many know too much.

MARIE VON EBNER-ESCHENBACH

What the mind doesn't understand it worships or fears.

ALICE WALKER

When knowledge comes in at the door, fear and superstition fly out of the window.

MARY ROBERTS RINEHART

An educated man should know everything about something, and something about everything.

C.V. WEDGWOOD

Knowledge . . . always imposes responsibility.

W.M.L. JAY

Once you have discovered what is happening, you can't pretend not to know, you can't abdicate responsibility.

P.D. JAMES

Learning is always rebellion . . . . Every bit of new truth discovered is revolutionary to what was believed before.

MARGARET LEE RUNBECK

Content should involve knowledge for "use" rather than for "possession."

HAROLD G. SHANE
AND JUNE GRANT SHANE

Knowledge conquered by labor becomes a possession,—a property entirely our own. A greater vividness and permanency of impression is secured, and facts thus acquired become registered in the mind in a way that mere imparted information can never produce.

THOMAS CARLYLE

It's a great nuisance that knowledge can only be acquired by hard work.

W. SOMERSET MAUGHAM

Knowledge of what you love somehow comes to you; you don't have to read nor analyze nor study. If you love a thing enough, knowledge of it seeps into you, with particulars more real than any chart can furnish.

JESSAMYN WEST

Knowledge is much like dust—it sticks to one, one does not know how.

L.E. LANDON

If they make you go where learning is flying around, some of it is bound to light on you.

SATCHEL PAIGE

Since we can't know what knowledge will be most needed in the future, it is senseless to try to teach it in advance. Instead, we should try to turn out people who love learning so much and learn so well that they will be able to learn whatever needs to be learned.

JOHN HOLT

We're drowning in information and starving for knowledge.

RUTHERFORD D. ROGERS

Our feelings are our most genuine paths to knowledge.

AUDRE LORDE

You cannot know what you do not feel.

MARYA MANNES

It is not only by the questions we have answered that progress may be measured, but also by those we are still asking. The passionate controversies of one era are viewed as sterile preoccupations by another, for knowledge alters what we seek as well as what we find.

FREDA ADLER

The person who knows it all has lots to learn.

ANONYMOUS

It's what you learn after you know it all that counts.

JOHN WOODEN

*W*ISDOM

Knowledge comes, but wisdom lingers.

ALFRED, LORD TENNYSON

Knowledge is proud that he has learned so much;
Wisdom is humble that he does not know more.

WILLIAM COWPER

Knowledge can be communicated, but not wisdom.
One can find it, live it, be fortified by it, do wonders
through it, but one cannot communicate and teach it.

HERMANN HESSE

Authority without wisdom is like a heavy axe without an edge, fitter to bruise than polish.

ANNE BRADSTREET

Learning without wisdom is a load of books on a donkey's back.

ZORA NEALE HURSTON

Much learning does not teach understanding.

HERACLITUS

We are wise so long as we seek wisdom. The moment we think we have found it, we become fools.

ANONYMOUS

It is well for us to realize that the great increase in knowledge in the world does not necessarily make us better or wiser. . . . A clever monkey may learn to drive a car, but he is hardly a safe chauffeur.

JAWAHARLAL NEHRU

The essence of wisdom is emancipation, as far as possible, from the tyranny of the here and the now.

BERTRAND RUSSELL

Not all clever words are true. . . . And inversely most things that are true are not clever.

BESS STREETER ALDRICH

The art of being wise is the art of knowing what to overlook.

WILLIAM JAMES

The first key to wisdom is this—constant and frequent questioning . . . for by doubting we are led to question and by questioning we arrive at the truth.

PETER ABELARD

There is only one way to wisdom: awe. . . . The loss of awe is the great block to insight . . . . The greatest insights happen to us in moments of awe.

ABRAHAM JOSHUA HESCHEL

With every increase of knowledge and skill, wisdom becomes more necessary, for every such increase augments our capacity for realizing our purposes, and therefore augments our capacity for evil, if our purposes are unwise. The world needs wisdom as it has never needed it before; and if knowledge continues to increase, the world will need wisdom in the future even more than it does now.

BERTRAND RUSSELL

A time has come in our history when what is known has little connection with what is done.

JENNIFER STONE

Some folks are wise, and some are otherwise.

TOBIAS SMOLLETT

CREATIVITY

The shrewd guess, the fertile hypothesis, the courageous leap to a tentative conclusion—these are the most valuable coins of the thinker at work. But in most schools guessing is heavily penalized and is associated somehow with laziness.

JEROME BRUNER

Those who have been required to memorize the world as it is will never create the world as it might be.

JUDITH GROCH

Sparks electric only strike
On souls electrical alike;
The flash of intellect expires,
Unless it meet congenial fires.

HANNAH MORE

You cannot create genius. All you can do is
nurture it.

NINETTE DE VALOIS

Perhaps the best thing we can do for the creative
person is to stay out of his way.

JUDITH GROCH

In this country we encourage "creativity" among the mediocre, but real bursting creativity appalls us. We put it down as undisciplined, as somehow "too much."

PAULINE KAEL

All children are artists, and it is an indictment of our culture that so many of them lose their creativity, their unfettered imaginations, as they grow older.

MADELEINE L'ENGLE

Creativity can be described as letting go of certainties.

GAIL SHEEHY

Little minds are interested in the extraordinary; great minds in the commonplace.

ELBERT HUBBARD

Our fundamental task as human beings is to seek out connections—to exercise our imaginations. It follows, then, that the basic task of education is the care and feeding of the imagination.

KATHERINE PATERSON

Imagination is more important than knowledge.

ALBERT EINSTEIN

Imagination! who can sing thy force?
Or who describe the swiftness of thy course?

PHILLIS WHEATLEY

Imagination is the highest kite that can fly.

LAUREN BACALL

The Possible's slow fuse is lit
By the Imagination.

EMILY DICKINSON

The imagination needs moodling,—long, ineffi-
cient, happy idling, dawdling and puttering.

BRENDA UELAND

Imagination is new reality in the process of being
created. It represents the part of the existing order
that can still grow.

NANCY HALE

I doubt the imagination can be suppressed. If you
truly eradicated it in a child, that child would grow
up to be an eggplant.

URSULA K. LE GUIN

URIOSITY

A sense of curiosity is nature's original school of education.

SMILEY BLANTON

Why—why—why! . . . Ask it of everything your mind touches, and let your mind touch everything!

ANN FAIRBAIRN

Learning is by nature curiosity . . . prying into everything, reluctant to leave anything, material or immaterial, unexplained.

PHILO

I think, at a child's birth, if a mother could ask a fairy godmother to endow it with the most useful gift, that gift should be curiosity.

ELEANOR ROOSEVELT

Curiosity is one of the permanent and certain characteristics of a vigorous mind.

SAMUEL JOHNSON

Curiosity is the one thing invincible in Nature.

FREYA STARK

Curiosity is one of those insatiable passions that grow by gratification.

SARAH SCOTT

Curiosity needs food as much as any of us, and dies soon if denied it.

STELLA BENSON

Some men and women are inquisitive about everything, they are always asking, if they see any one with anything they ask what is that thing, what is it you are carrying, what are you going to be doing with that thing, why have you that thing, where did you get that thing, how long will you have that thing, there are very many men and women who want to know about anything about everything.

GERTRUDE STEIN

People say: idle curiosity. The one thing that curiosity cannot be is idle.

LEO ROSTEN

Worlds can be found by a child and an adult bending down and looking together under the grass stems or at the skittering crabs in a tidal pool.

MARY CATHERINE BATESON

The days on which one has been most inquisitive are among the days on which one has been happiest.

ROBERT LYND

Children are notoriously curious about everything— everything except . . . the things people want them to know. It then remains for us to refrain from forcing any kind of knowledge upon them, and they will be curious about everything.

FLOYD DELL

EADING

Reading is to the mind what exercise is to the body.

JOSEPH ADDISON

Trusting children and books is a revolutionary act. Books are, after all, dangerous stuff. Leave a child alone with a book and you don't know what might happen.

SUSAN OHANIAN

There is no substitute for books in the life of a child.

MARY ELLEN CHASE

Books, to the reading child, are so much more than books—they are dreams and knowledge, they are a future, and a past.

ESTHER MEYNELL

Make it a rule never to give a child a book you would not read yourself.

GEORGE BERNARD SHAW

In recommending a book . . . the less said the better. The moment you praise a book too highly you awaken resistance in your listener.

HENRY MILLER

It would be a good idea if children would write books for older people, now that everyone is writing for children.

G.C. LICHTENBERG

As a child I felt that books were holy objects, to be caressed, rapturously sniffed, and devotedly provided for. I gave my life to them—I still do. I continue to do what I did as a child: dream of books, make books, and collect books.

MAURICE SENDAK

As a little girl my greatest joy was to lose myself in a book—at first it was books with big pictures and few words and gradually books with many words and few or no pictures . . . . Today, many years later and millions of words later, I still get a positively physical pleasure from a beautifully carved sentence or a powerfully expressed idea.

ARIANNA STASSINOPOULOS

Learning is a stove plant that lives in the cottage and thrives during the long winter in domestic warmth. Unless it be borne into children in their earliest years, there is little hope for it. The whole future of civilization depends upon what is read to children before they can read to themselves.

JOHN JAY CHAPMAN

Children are made readers on the laps of their parents.

EMILIE BUCHWALD

The influence of early books is profound. So much of the future lies on the shelves; early reading has more influence on the conduct than any religious teaching.

GRAHAM GREENE

There are books that one needs maturity to enjoy just as there are books an adult can come on too late to savor.

PHYLLIS MCGINLEY

When I was about eight, I decided that the most wonderful thing, next to a human being, was a book.

MARGARET WALKER

I do not know how I learned to read. I only remember my first books and their effect upon me; it is from my earliest reading that I date the unbroken consciousness of my own existence.

JEAN-JACQUES ROUSSEAU

The first book that a child reads has a colossal impact.

JOAN AIKEN

We are made whole
By books, as by great spaces and the stars.

MARY CAROLYN DAVIES

I've never known any trouble that an hour's reading didn't assuage.

MONTESQUIEU

I pity those who have no taste for reading.

MADAME DE SÉVIGNÉ

Readers are lucky—they will never be bored or lonely.

NATALIE BABBITT

A room without books is like a body without a soul.

CICERO

A house without books is like a room without windows.

HORACE MANN

Books are the carriers of civilization. Without books, history is silent, literature dumb, science crippled, thought and speculation at a standstill.

BARBARA W. TUCHMAN

The man who does not read good books has no advantage over the man who can't read them.

MARK TWAIN

When I get a little money, I buy books; and if any is left, I buy food and clothes.

ERASMUS

I cannot live without books.

THOMAS JEFFERSON

Next to acquiring good friends, the best acquisition is that of good books.

CHARLES CALEB COLTON

It is a good thing to start life with a small number of really good books which are your very own.

SIR ARTHUR CONAN DOYLE

Do not read good books—life is too short for that—only read the best.

ERNEST DIMNET

Life being very short, and the quiet hours of it few, we ought to waste none of them in reading valueless books.

JOHN RUSKIN

Since each child reads only about six hundred books in the course of childhood, each book should nourish them in some way—with new ideas, insight, humor, or vocabulary.

JOAN AIKEN

Never read a book through merely because you have begun it.

JOHN WITHERSPOON

No entertainment is so cheap as reading, nor any pleasure so lasting.

LADY MARY WORTLEY MONTAGU

Some of the sweetest hours of life, on retrospect, will be found to have been spent with books.

RALPH WALDO EMERSON

Only one hour in the normal day is more pleasurable than the hour spent in bed with a book before going to sleep, and that is the hour spent in bed with a book after being called in the morning.

ROSE MACAULAY

I only really love a book when I have read it at least four times.

NANCY SPAIN

The greatest pleasures of reading consist in
re-reading.

VERNON LEE

Men must read for amusement as well as for
knowledge.

HENRY WARD BEECHER

Only read what gives you the greatest pleasure.

ERNEST DIMNET

A man ought to read just as inclination leads him;
for what he reads as a task will do him little good.

SAMUEL JOHNSON

I believe that any book, however trashy and ephemeral, is good for a child if he finds pleasure in reading it. Any book that helps him to form a habit of reading, that helps to make reading one of his deep and continuing needs, is good for him.

RICHARD MCKENNA

Children read to *learn*—even when they are reading fantasy, nonsense, light verse, comics, or the copy on cereal packets, they are expanding their minds all the time, enlarging their vocabulary, making discoveries; it is all new to them.

JOAN AIKEN

The sum of it all is: read what you like, because you like it, seeking no other reason and no other profit than the experience of reading.

HOLBROOK JACKSON

Whatever we read from intense curiosity gives us
the model of how we should always read. Plodding
along page after page with an equal attention to
each word results in attention to mere words.

ERNEST DIMNET

What blockheads are those wise persons, who think
it necessary that a child should comprehend everything it reads.

ROBERT SOUTHEY

It is desultory reading that develops one's taste. It is
fortunate that when we are young we are unfocused.

VAN WYCK BROOKS

It's such a wonderful feeling to watch a child discover that reading is a marvelous adventure rather than a chore.

ZILPHA KEATLEY SNYDER

The book which you read from a sense of duty, or because for any reason you must, does not commonly make friends with you. It may happen that it will yield you an unexpected delight, but this will be in its own unentreated way in spite of your good intentions.

WILLIAM DEAN HOWELLS

The foolishest book is a kind of leaky boat on a sea of wisdom; some of the wisdom will get in anyhow.

OLIVER WENDELL HOLMES, SR.

The greatest gift is the passion for reading. It is cheap, it consoles, it distracts, it excites, it gives you knowledge of the world and experience of a wide kind. It is a moral illumination.

ELIZABETH HARDWICK

Those who are happy enough to have a taste for reading, need never be at a loss for amusement.

MADAME DE SÉVIGNÉ

A good book has no ending.

R.D. CUMMING

It is not true that we have only one life to live; if we can read we can live as many more lives and as many kinds as we wish.

S.I. HAYAKAWA

We live at the level of our language. Whatever we can articulate we can imagine or understand or explore. All you have to do to educate a child is leave him alone and teach him to read. The rest is brainwashing.

ELLEN GILCHRIST

Teaching children to read was one thing; keeping them interested in reading was something else.

MARVA COLLINS

If you wish to be a good reader, read.

EPICTETUS

Fitting people with books is about as difficult as fitting them with shoes.

SYLVIA BEACH

Let us secure not such books as people want, but books just above their wants, and they will reach up to take what is put out for them.

MARIA MITCHELL

As you grow ready for it, somewhere or other you will find what is needful for you in a book.

GEORGE MACDONALD

Books are teachers. Good books go right on instructing in odd moments when the teachers and parents are not on duty.

ANONYMOUS

The real purpose of books is to trap the mind into doing its own thinking.

CHRISTOPHER MORLEY

Children have a lot more to worry about from the parents who raised them than from the books they read.

E.L. DOCTOROW

My education was the liberty I had to read indiscriminately and all the time with my eyes hanging out.

DYLAN THOMAS

Some books are to be tasted, others to be swallowed, and some few to be chewed and digested.

FRANCIS BACON

To read without reflecting is like eating without digesting.

EDMUND BURKE

Education . . . has produced a vast population able to read but unable to distinguish what is worth reading.

GEORGE MACAULAY TREVELYAN

Of all the nations in the Western world, the United States, with the most money and the most time, has the fewest readers of books per capita. This is an incalculable loss.

ELEANOR ROOSEVELT

The trouble with education is that we always read everything when we're too young to know what it means. And the trouble with life is that we're always too busy to re-read it later.

MARGARET BARNES

We could revolutionize education if we asked every person connected with the education of children, "Read any good books lately?"

SUSAN OHANIAN

The wonderful thing about books is that they allow us to enter imaginatively into someone else's life. And when we do that, we learn to sympathize with other people. But the real surprise is that we also learn truths about ourselves, about our own lives, that somehow we hadn't been able to see before.

KATHERINE PATERSON

We need the slower and more lasting stimulus of solitary reading as a relief from the pressure on eye, ear and nerves of the torrent of information and entertainment pouring from ever-open electronic jaws. It could end by stupefying us.

STORM JAMESON

NOT READING

Children who can't get themselves out of bed on a school day will be up by 5 a.m. to watch Saturday morning cartoons.

LISA COFIELD, DEBBIE DINGERSON, AND LEA RUSH

The six and one-fourth hours' television watching (the American average per day) which non-reading children do is what is called alpha-level learning. The mind needn't make any pictures since the pictures are provided, so the mind cuts current as low as it can.

CAROL BLY

The students are used to being entertained. They are used to the idea that if they are just the slightest bit bored, they can flip the switch and turn the channel.

IRENE KRAMSKY

[Television viewing] is a one-way transaction that requires the taking in of particular sensory material in a particular way, no matter what the material might be. There is, indeed, no other experience in a child's life that permits quite so much intake while demanding so little outflow.

MARIE WINN

Until a child can meet reality, he must live in fantasy. But he must create his own fantasy. And it is television's primary damage that it provides ten million children with the same fantasy, ready-made and on a platter.

MARYA MANNES

McLuhanism and the media have broken the back of the book business; they've freed people from the shame of not reading. They've rationalized becoming stupid and watching television.

PAULINE KAEL

Even if every program were educational and every
advertisement bore the seal of approval of the
American Dental Association, we would still have a
critical problem. It's not just the programs but the
act of watching television hour after hour after hour
that's destructive.

ELLEN GOODMAN

To a certain extent the child's early television experiences will serve to dehumanize, to mechanize, to
make less *real* the realities and relationships he
encounters in life. For him, real events will always
carry subtle echoes of the television world.

MARIE WINN

TV is a language all its own, a land of one dimen-
sional stereotypes that destroys culture, not adds to it.
TV is anti-art, a reflection of consumerism that serves
the power structure. TV is about demographics.

ROSEANNE BARR

Children who have been taught, or conditioned, to listen passively most of the day to the warm verbal communications coming from the TV screen, to the deep emotional appeal of the so-called TV personality, are often unable to respond to real persons because they arouse so much less feeling than the skilled actor.

Bruno Bettelheim

Television and radio violence was considered by most experts of minimal importance as a contributory cause of youthful killing. . . . There were always enough experts to assure the public that crime and violence had nothing to do with crime and violence.

Marya Mannes

The American child, driven to school by bus and stupefied by television, is losing contact with reality. There is an enormous gap between the sheer weight of the textbooks that he carries home from school and his capacity to interpret what is in them.

MARGUERITE YOURCENAR

Educational television should be absolutely forbidden. It can only lead to unreasonable expectations and eventual disappointment when your child discovers that the letters of the alphabet do not leap up out of books and dance around the room with royal-blue chickens.

FRAN LEBOWITZ